CONTENTS

Drawing Tools

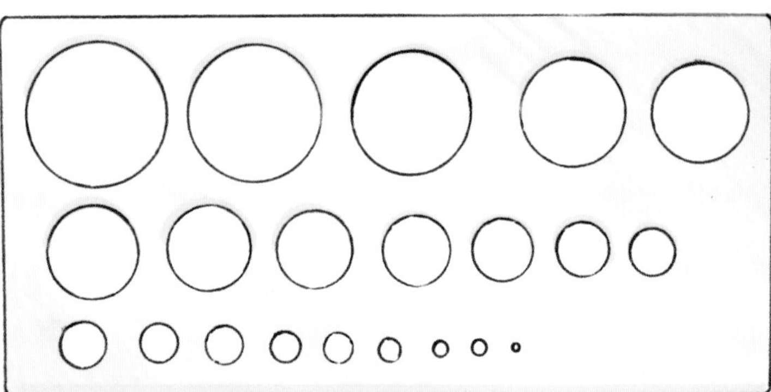

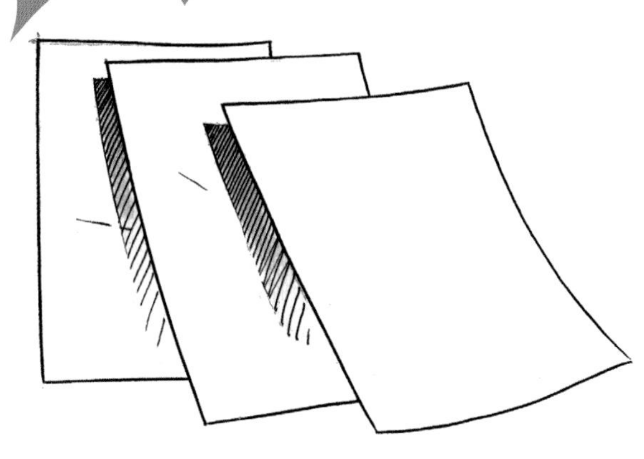

LAYOUT PAPER

Most professional illustrators use cheaper paper for basic layouts and practice sketches before they get around to the more serious task of producing a masterpiece on more costly paper. It's a good idea to buy some plain paper from a stationery shop for all your practice sketches. Go for the least expensive kind.

DRAWING PAPER

This is a heavy-duty, high-quality paper, ideal for your final version. You don't have to buy the most expensive brand. Most decent art or craft shops stock their own brand or a student brand and, unless you're thinking of turning professional, these will be fine.

WATERCOLOUR PAPER

This paper is made from 100 per cent cotton and is much higher quality than wood-based papers. Most art shops stock a large range of weights and sizes. Paper that is 300 gsm (140 lb) should be fine.

CIRCLE TEMPLATE

This is very useful for drawing small circles.

FRENCH CURVES

These are available in a few shapes and sizes and are useful for drawing curves.

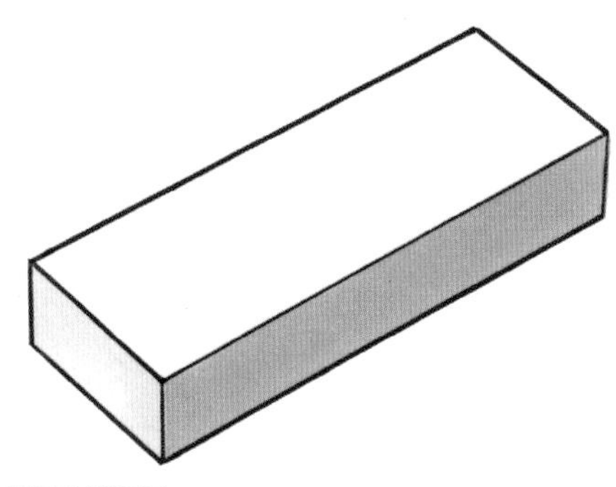

ERASER

There are three main types of eraser: rubber, plastic and putty. Try all three to see which kind you prefer.

HOW C NOVEL

A N
IN YOUR GRAPHIC NOVEL

FRANK LEE

W
FRANKLIN WATTS
LONDON • SYDNEY

First published in 2012 by Franklin Watts

Franklin Watts
338 Euston Road
London NW1 3BH

Franklin Watts Australia
Level 17/207 Kent Street, Sydney, NSW 2000

Produced by Arcturus Publishing Limited,
26/27 Bickels Yard, 151–153 Bermondsey Street, London SE1 3HA

Text and illustrations: Frank Lee with Jim Hansen and Peter Gray
Editors: Joe Harris and Kate Overy
Design: Andrew Easton
Cover design: Andrew Easton

A CIP catalogue record for this book is available from the British Library.

Dewey Decimal Classification Number 741.5'1

ISBN: 978 1 4451 1028 8

Printed in China

Franklin Watts is a division of Hachette Children's Books, an Hachette UK company.
www.hachette.co.uk

SLOO2O68EN
Supplier O3, Date O112, Print Run 1418

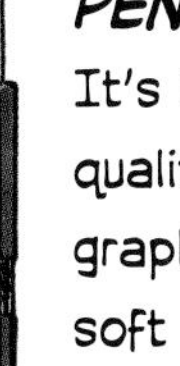

PENCILS

It's best not to cut corners on quality here. Get a good range of graphite (lead) pencils ranging from soft (B) to hard (2H).

Hard lead lasts longer and leaves less graphite on the paper. Soft lead leaves more lead on the paper and wears down more quickly. Every artist has their personal preference, but H pencils are a good medium range to start out with until you find your favourite.

Spend some time drawing with each weight of pencil and get used to their different qualities. Another good product to try is the mechanical pencil. These are available in a range of lead thicknesses, 0.5 mm being a good medium range. These pencils are very good for fine detail work.

BRUSHES

Some artists like to use a fine brush for inking linework. This takes a bit more practice and patience to master, but the results can be very satisfying. If you want to try your hand at brushwork, you will definitely need to get some good-quality sable brushes.

MARKERS

These are very versatile pens and, with practice, can give pleasing results.

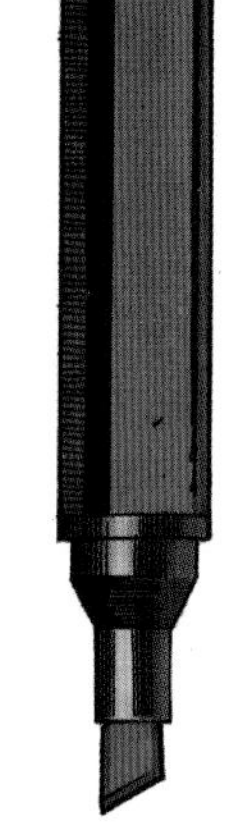

PENS

There is a large range of good-quality pens on the market these days and all will do a decent job of inking. It's important to experiment with different pens to determine which you are most comfortable using.

You may find that you end up using a combination of pens to produce your finished artwork. Remember to use a pen that has waterproof ink if you want to colour your illustration with a watercolour or ink wash. It's a good idea to use one of these anyway. There's nothing worse than having your nicely inked drawing ruined by an accidental drop of water!

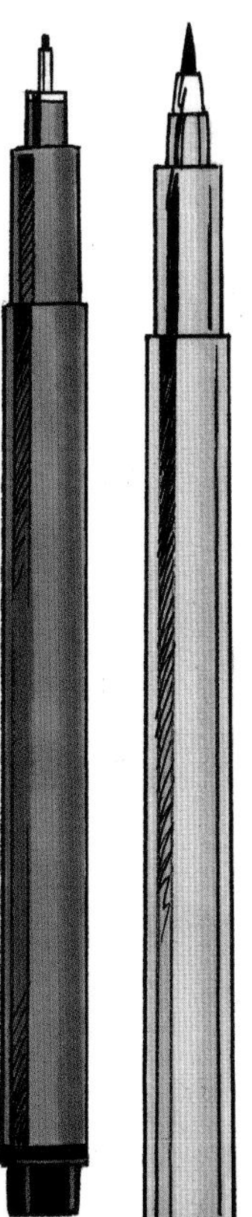

INKS

With the dawn of computers and digital illustration, materials such as inks have become a bit obscure, so you may have to look harder for these. Most good art and craft shops should stock them, though.

Dynamic Poses

This book is all about action. You will learn how to make your comic-book panels and covers more interesting by animating your characters. As you develop your figure-drawing skills, you will be able to transform simple stances into explosive action poses!

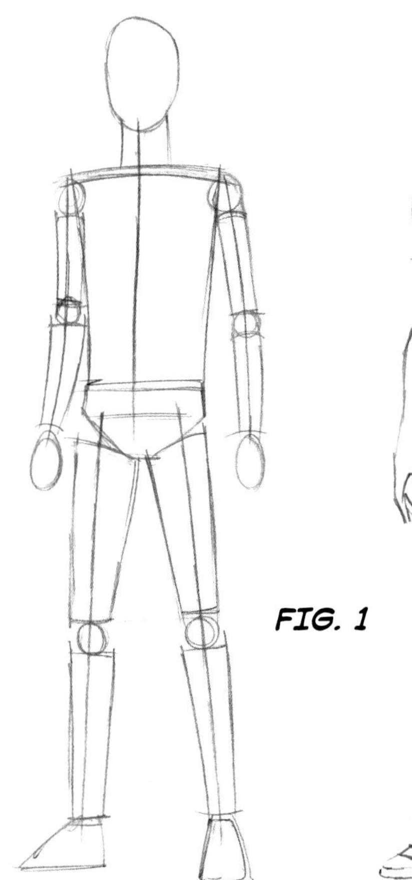

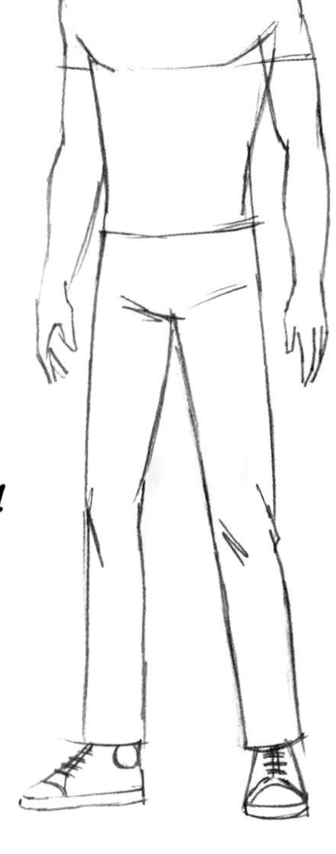

FIG. 1

Standing Ready

Take a look at the two figures on this page. The first character (Fig. 1) is standing in a lifeless, uninteresting pose. However, the second character (Fig. 2) looks ready for action. Look at the construction diagrams that show how the two figures were composed, and you'll see some important differences. Even if your character is just standing still, the use of dynamic figure poses brings him to life. This will make your comic-book pages look more much exciting.

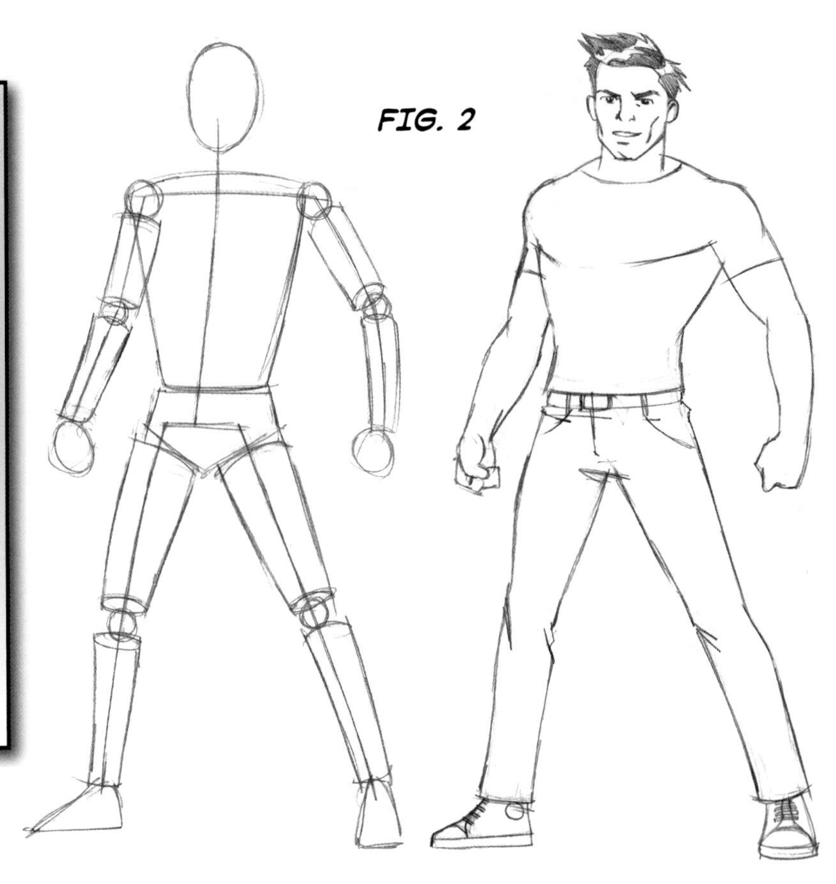

FIG. 2

Acting the Part

Imagine that you are a director and your characters are actors. What does their performance tell us? These two characters may be standing still, but their poses tell us immediately that they are confident and powerful.

Strike a Pose!

The barbarian (above) has his legs spread wide and holds his arms away from his body. This tells us he is ready for battle. The superheroine (right) has her hands on her hips and one knee bent. This tells us she is sassy and self-assured.

Running: Front View

Let's get moving! Here are some running poses viewed from the front. The second version (Fig. 2) is more dynamic. You can really feel the action. It looks like the figure could leap off the page towards you! Try to choose poses that feel high-powered and energetic. These will make your graphic novel feel action-packed.

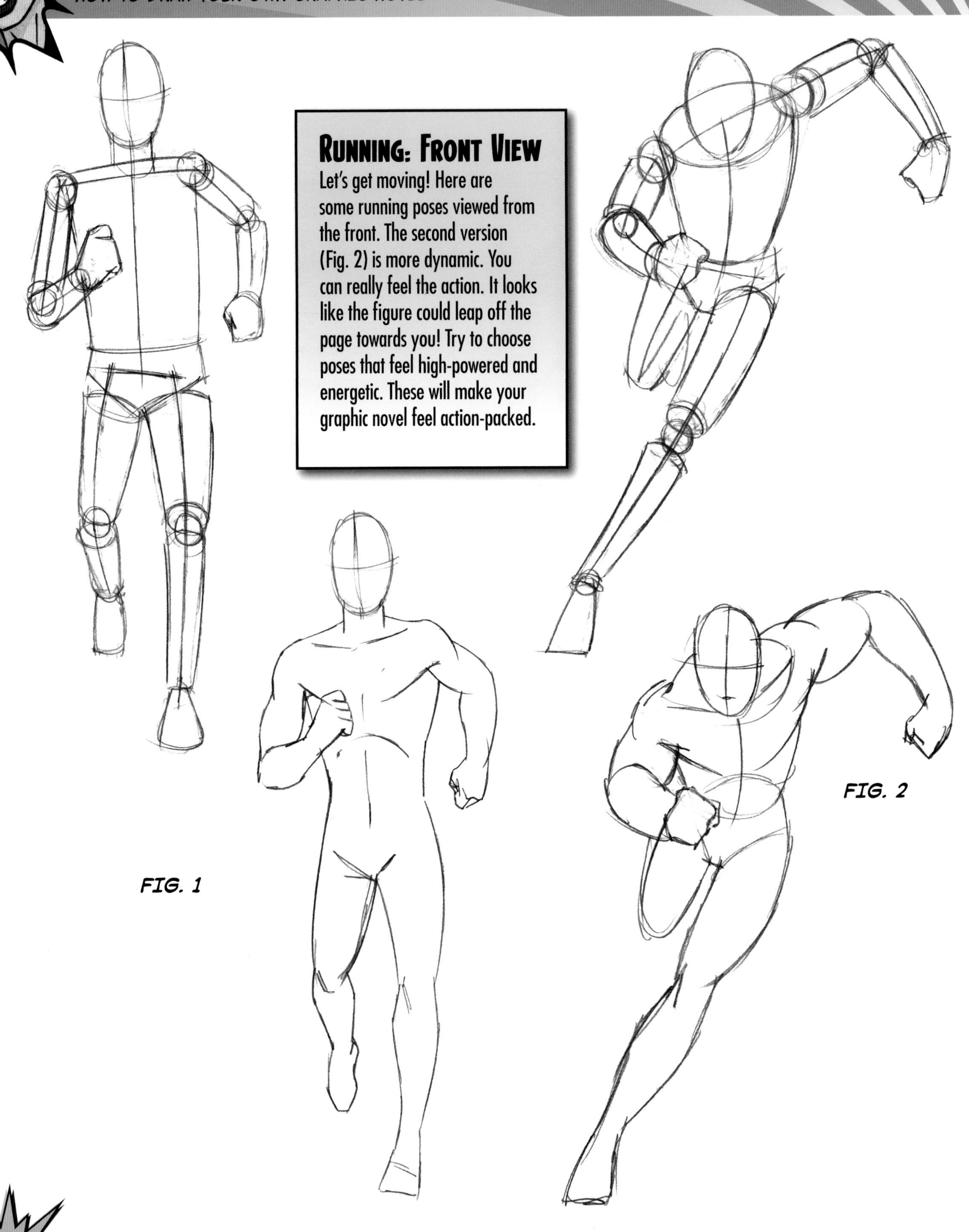

FIG. 1

FIG. 2

Running: Side View

Look at the images of two different side-view running poses below. Which one do you find more interesting? The figure in a casual running pose on the left (Fig. 1)? Or the figure on the right who looks like he's about to take off (Fig. 2)? No contest! Sometimes it helps to start off with a more boring pose then exaggerate the action you're drawing gradually, in stages, until you end up with a really exciting pose.

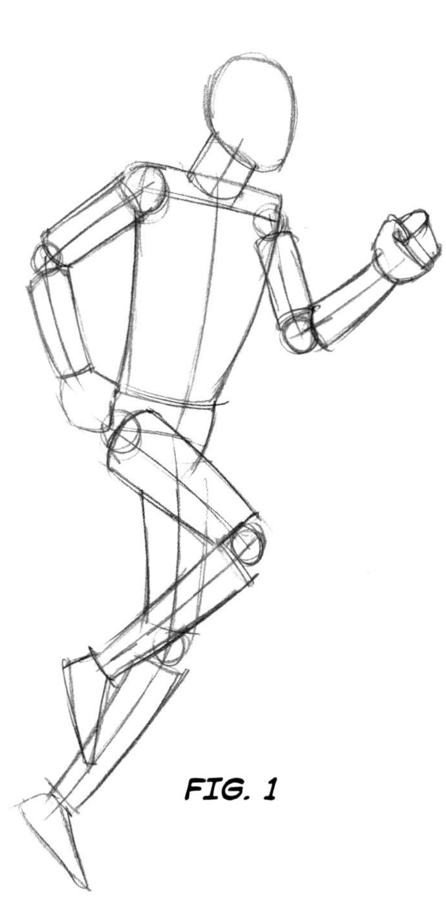

FIG. 1

FIG. 2

Step by Step: Run For It!

Here's a step-by-step guide to drawing, inking and colouring a running character. The main thing about this pose is that it's not balanced. If you tried to stand like this yourself, you would fall over. That imbalance helps give the impression of movement.

STEP 1

Draw the character's head, chest and pelvis first. You are drawing her body from the side but with it leaning forward so the body parts follow a diagonal line. Now add the limbs.

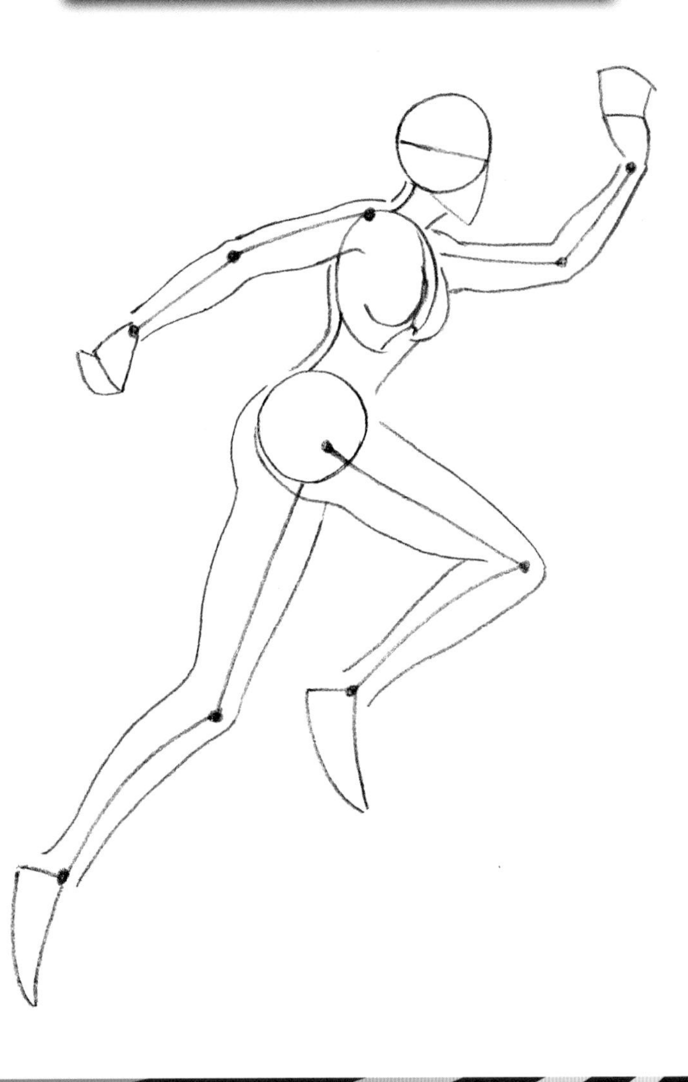

STEP 2

Draw the outline shape of her flesh and muscle. Notice how there are strong curves in the shape at the backs of the legs to show her strong muscles.

STEP 3

Add some basic lines for her tunic and cloak. Add the main features of the face and some of the curves of the hair. Work on the shape of the feet.

STEP 4

Give the clothing more detail. Notice the square-shaped neck of the tunic. Draw some lines along the bottom of the skirt and cloak to show the folds. Work on the hands and feet. She is wearing sandals, so you'll still be able to see her toes in the final picture.

STEP 5

Once you're happy with your drawing, go over your pencil lines in ink. Now add some shading to the hair to give it more depth.

STEP 6

Leave the ink to dry, then erase all your remaining pencil guidelines.

STEP 7

Now you can add some colour to your picture. We've given her auburn hair and a green tunic. Notice how dark the inside of the cloak is where it is in shadow.

Fighting Poses

If you plan to show your heroes and villains in conflict, you'll need to learn how to draw combat poses.

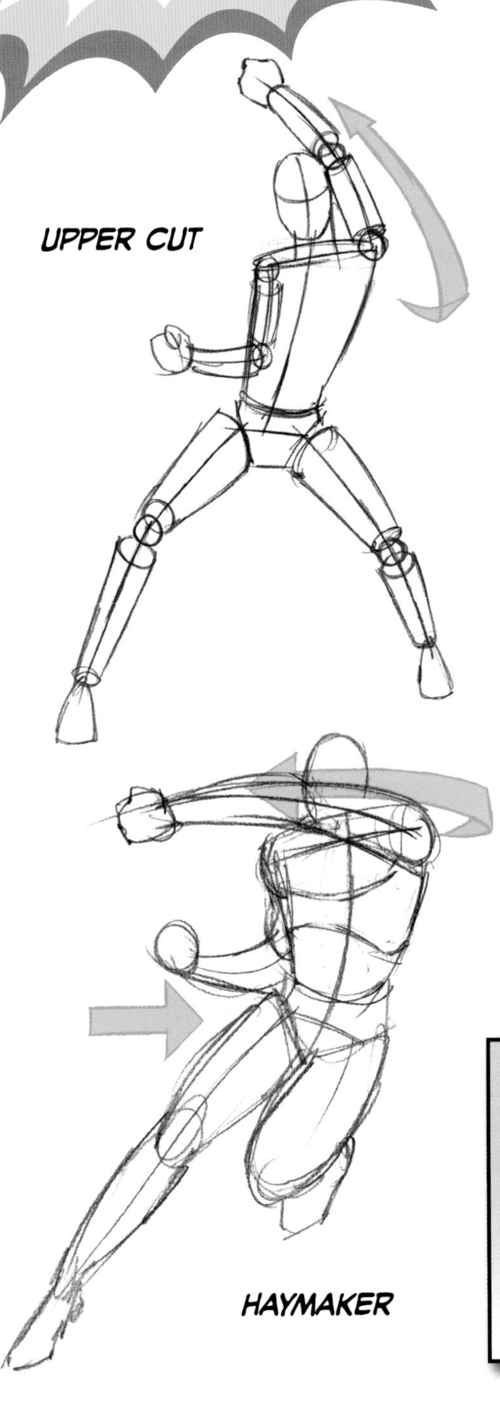

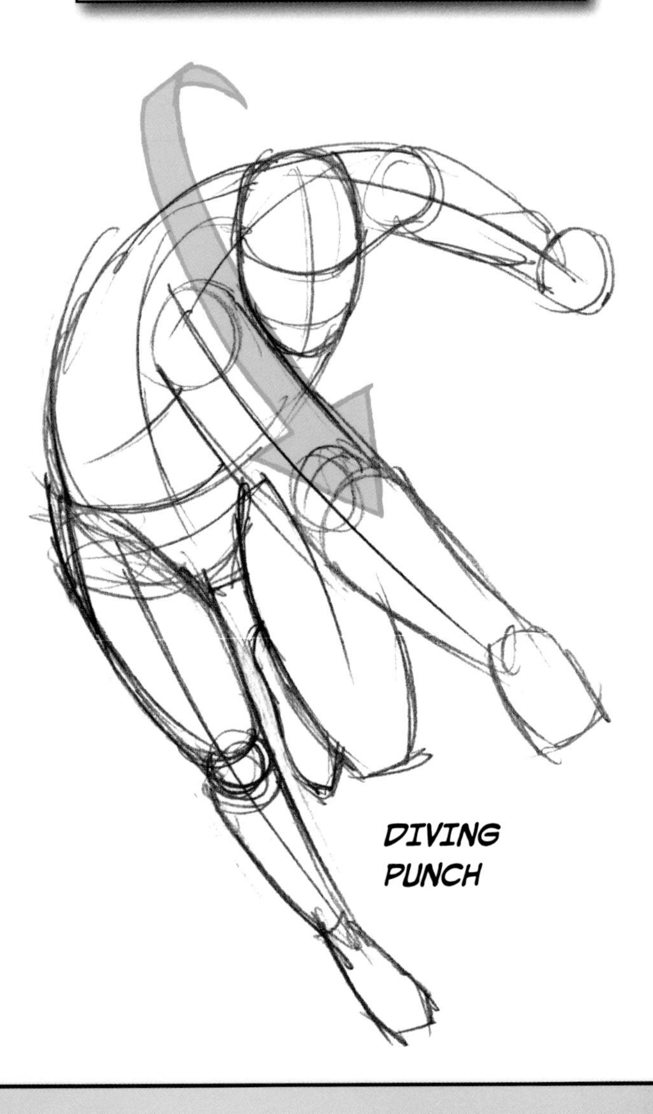

Punching

To draw a really convincing punch, you have to consider the flow and direction of the action. Look at the three different examples on this page. Arrows have been added to show the flow of action through the body.

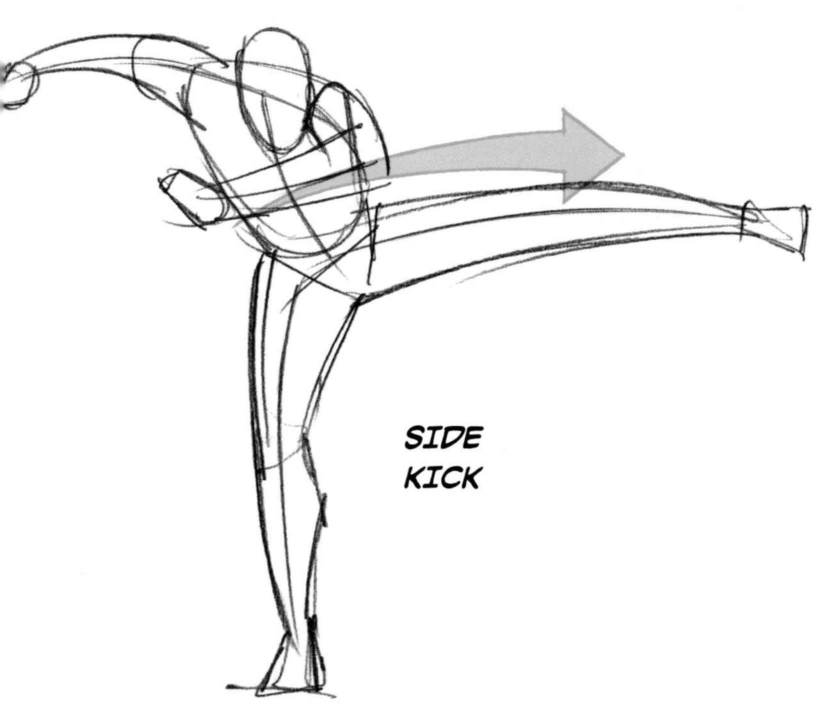

KICKING

Here we have some different types of dynamic kicking actions. Characters trained in martial arts are often seen in kicking poses. These poses show off their skills in the art of combat. Each of these figures is delivering a different type of kick.

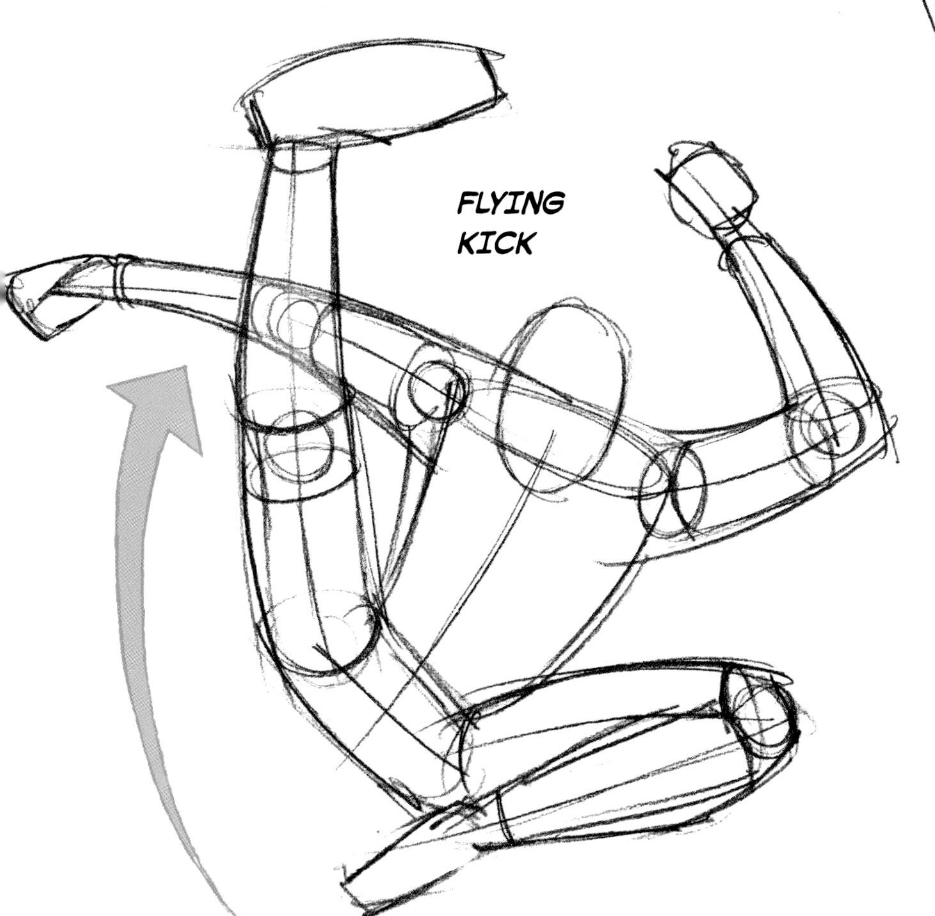

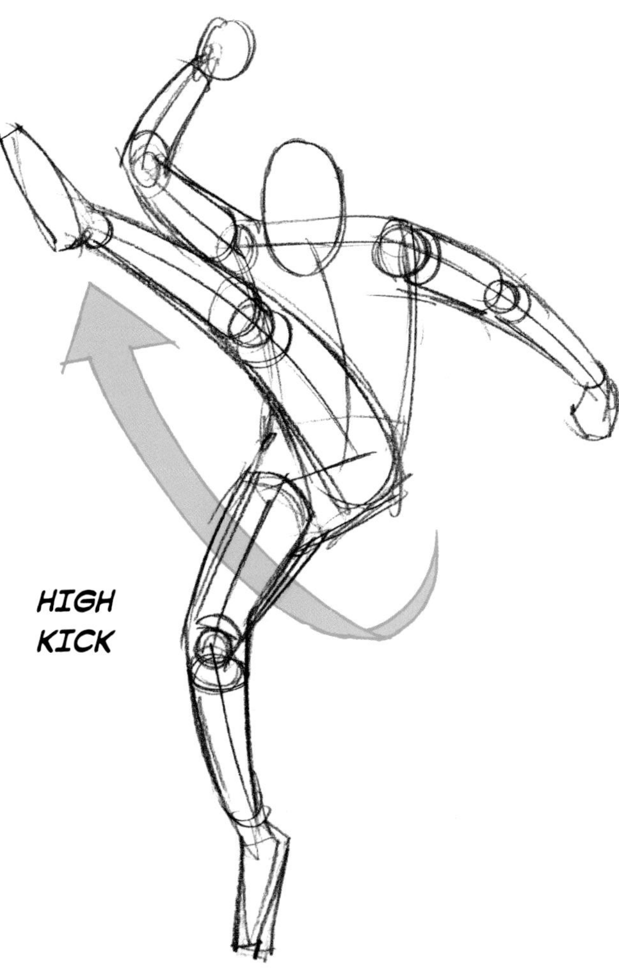

Step by Step: Fighting Hero

This hero has his right hand pulled back, ready to deliver a wall-smashing punch.

STEP 1
Start by creating the loose, skeletal stick figure.

STEP 2
Start to flesh out the figure using the construction shapes.

STEP 3
Now begin to develop the outer form of the figure, adding basic muscle detail. At this stage you should keep your pencil sketch loose and light.

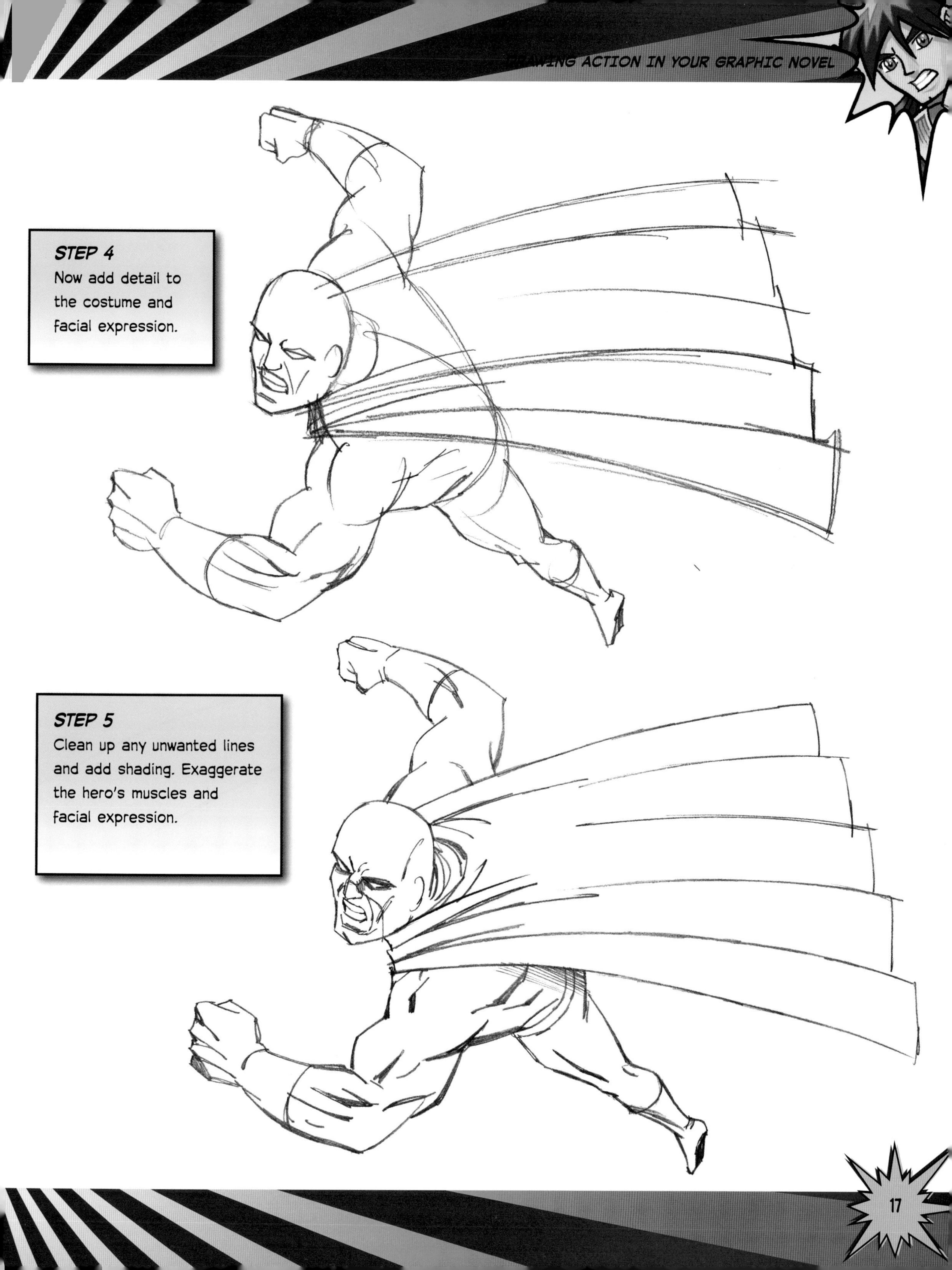

STEP 4
Now add detail to the costume and facial expression.

STEP 5
Clean up any unwanted lines and add shading. Exaggerate the hero's muscles and facial expression.

STEP 6

Find the strongest pencil lines and go over them in ink. Add darker areas to define his muscles and to give his cape more weight.

STEP 7

The hero's cape billows out behind him as he lunges forward. This gives the image a real sense of movement. Individually shade each fold of the cape to make it look three-dimensional.

MORE ACTION POSES

LOOSEN UP!

To create strong action poses, you must feel the action. Don't draw too carefully at first or you will end up with a stiff pose. Start with a series of loose sketches. It doesn't matter if you don't produce a perfect drawing right away.

Jumping and Leaping

Whether it's to show your superhero leaping into action to save someone in danger or your bad guy pouncing in attack, you need to know how to draw all sorts of different jumping poses. All the poses shown here have a strong directional movement. It might take several attempts to get the right pose, but it's worth the effort.

Weapons in Action

Here we have a series of action poses showing combat using a weapon. Think about the direction of the action and then make your character's body follow it. The key is to capture a dramatic movement in a few simple lines. Once you have captured the flow of action, you can refine the figure by adding more detail.

Showing Speed

How can you show that something is happening quickly when your images are static? The answer is speed lines. These are a great way of conveying not just rapid movement, but also intensity and power.

Radial speed lines (such as in the image above) give a feeling of forward or backward movement. Speed lines can also be horizontal, angular or vertical (see below).

HORIZONTAL

AT AN ANGLE (FOLLOW THE LINES OF PERSPECTIVE)

VERTICAL

The key to drawing great action is to capture a dramatic movement in a few simple lines. Once you have captured the flow of action, you can refine the figure by adding more detail. At this stage you can make sure the proportions are correct.

Our first character is built around two lines (in red) shaped like an X.

This second character has a simple diagonal line as his starting point.

Capes and hair can play an important role in creating a sense of flowing, directional movement.

Step by Step: Flying Heroine

Superhero characters should look like they are in dynamic movement as they fly.

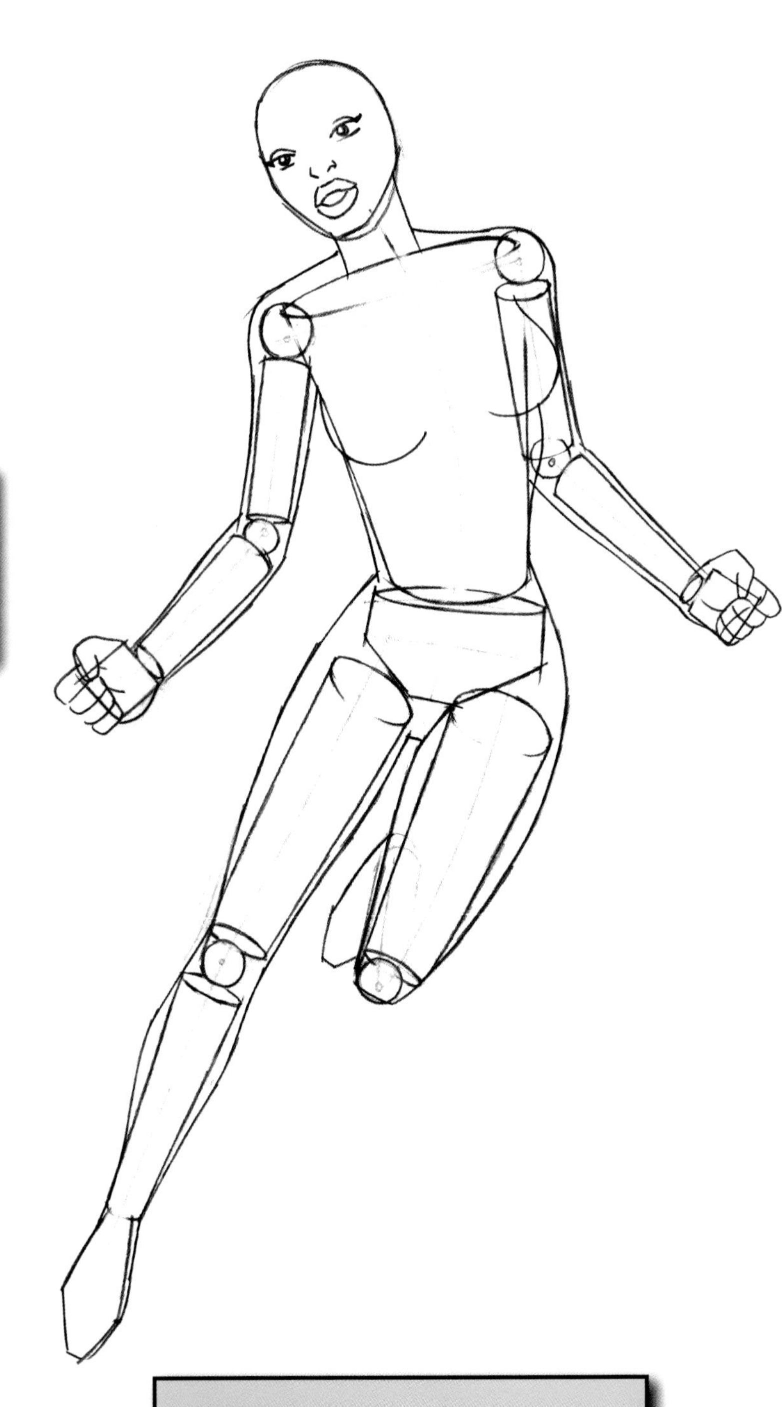

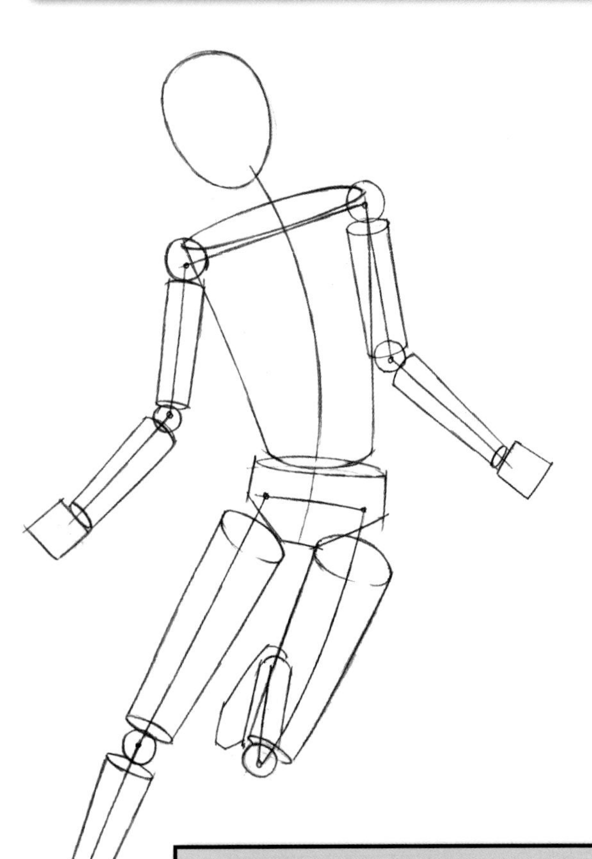

STEP 1
Draw the superheroine's flying pose using a stick figure, then build on it with the basic construction shapes.

STEP 2
Add the facial features and define the figure by smoothing out the construction shapes. When you are happy with how it looks, draw an outline around the shapes.

STEP 3

Once you have defined the shape of the body, remove your rough lines and shapes and start penciling in her costume. We've chosen a classic superhero style – a spandex suit, a cape and a mask.

STEP 4

Clean up the pencil work and add any final details. Shade in any areas that will be inked in solid black.

STEP 5

Now carefully ink over your pencil work to make your drawing bolder.

STEP 6

Choose a colour scheme that complements the character, using a palette that's pleasing to the eye. We have chosen a simple two-colour scheme of red and yellow, but there are endless possibilities! Try adapting the colours and suit design to create your own superheroine!

construction shapes Shapes such as blocks and balls, which are drawn over a stick figure to make it more three-dimensional.

directional movement In a drawing, this is the impression that a figure is moving in a certain direction, such as forward and out of the page towards the reader.

director The person who decides how a film or stage play should be performed. For example, the director tells actors how to move and what emotions they should recreate.

flow of action The movements that flow through a body during an action such as running or jumping.

layouts Sketches that show where items, such as figures and words, will be positioned on each page.

lines of perspective The angled lines in a drawing that give an impression of depth or distance.

matchstick figure A simple drawing of a person using sticks and circles.

proportions The sizes of different parts of a figure in comparison to each other. For example, the head should be sized according to the figure's height.

speed lines Drawn or painted lines (often in the background) that give the impression that an object or person is moving fast.

FURTHER READING

Draw Comic Book Action by Lee Garbett (Impact, 2010)

How to Draw Dynamic Comic Books by Rich Buckler (Vanguard, 2007)

Stan Lee's How to Draw Comics by Stan Lee (Watson-Guptill, 2010)

Write Your Own Graphic Novel by Natalie M Rosinsky (Capstone Press, 2009)

You Can Do a Graphic Novel by Barbara Slate (Alpha Books, 2010)

WEBSITES

Drawing Comics and Anime
www.drawcomics.net

Drawing Comics: Video Tutorials
http://www.ehow.com/video_4754254_draw-comics.html

Drawing Manga: Video Tutorials
http://www.youtube.com/user/markcrilley

INDEX